PUEBLO ARCHITECTURE
OF THE SOUTHWEST

a photographic essay

PUEBLO ARCHITECTURE OF THE SOUTHWEST

A PHOTOGRAPHIC ESSAY

photographs by William Current

text by Vincent Scully

Published for the Amon Carter Museum of Western Art, Fort Worth,

by the University of Texas Press, Austin and London

International Standard Book Number 0-292-70120-9
Library of Congress Catalog Card Number 70-146970
© 1971 by the Amon Carter Museum of Western Art
All Rights Reserved
Type set by Typoservice Corporation,
Indianapolis, Indiana
Printed by The Meriden Gravure Company,
Meriden, Connecticut
Bound by Universal Bookbindery, Inc.,
San Antonio, Texas

ILLUSTRATIONS

ACKNOWLEDGMENTS: I wish to express my appreciation to the John Simon Guggenheim Foundation and to John Szarkowski of the Museum of Modern Art for his encouragement.

W. C.
Pasadena

PREFACE

The ruins of the prehistoric pueblos of the Southwest and
their successors, the modern pueblos, with their incomparable dances, form a special cultural resource which is
not yet valued as it deserves to be throughout the United
States. General archaeological studies, with bibliogra-
phies listing specialized works and sources, include Alfred
Vincent Kidder, *An Introduction to the Study of Southwestern Archaeology* (New Haven : Yale University Press,
1924), new edition with a summary of southwestern
archaeology today by Irving Rouse (1962) ; H. M. Worm-
ington, *Prehistoric Indians of the Southwest,* The Denver
Museum of Natural History, Popular series no. 7 (Denver,
1961) ; and now Gordon R. Willey, *An Introduction to
American Archaeology,* Vol. I, *North and Middle America*
(Englewood Cliffs, N.J.: Prentice-Hall, 1966). For the
dances, about which much remains to be written, see
Erna Fergusson, *Dancing Gods: Indian Ceremonials of
New Mexico and Arizona* (Albuquerque : University of
New Mexico Press, 1931). Frank Waters, *Masked Gods:
Navaho and Pueblo Ceremonialism* (Denver, 1950), con-

tains many insights. My text here is intended only as a preliminary art historical introduction to the subject, insofar as Mr. Current's photographs can be used to serve that end. The captions supplement the text and have a few more specific things to say about the photographs themselves. I am indebted for much help and many kindnesses to Marjorie Lambert, George Ewing, Stewart Peckham, and the other scholars of the Anthropology Laboratory of the Museum of New Mexico. Philip Garvin has advised me in some problems of photographic criticism.

V. S.
Santa Fe and New Haven

PUEBLO ARCHITECTURE

OF THE SOUTHWEST

a photographic essay

INTRODUCTION

Wiliam Current's photographs endow the ruins of prehistoric Pueblo architecture with human immanence and emotional depth (Fig. 1). They are darkly printed and brooding in effect, but, perhaps in part for those very reasons, they alert us to the ghosts of the Anasazi, the Ancient Ones, who constructed the buildings, as if they might appear at any moment in the T-shaped doorways, so giving proper scale and value to the myriads of tiny stones.

One reason why Current is able to make the ruins real is his disciplined, even courageous, refusal to exploit the photographic technique with snappy views and tricky angles. He seems determined to be straightforward and to show the buildings as they exist in their environment. Using a camera with a square format almost all the time, he normally sticks to the proportions of his view finder with religious constancy. Perhaps because of all this directness, his photographs sometimes seem rather flat; no fancy lenses are involved. But their darkness has a richness in it, too, creating an effect in black and white which is almost that of color.

As a modern man with a photographer's pictorial eye, Current is also drawn to the more spectacular natural formations where some of the pueblos were built into the sides of cliffs (Figs. 2, 3). But here his art takes on sculptural qualities, and it makes us sense the earth more or less as the Indians regard it, as a physical presence, embodying fundamental force and divinity. Current's lens rubs the sky out white and plunges us into the archaic depths of the Canyon de Chelly (Fig. 2) or leads us across the rounded bosses of the cliffs which bound the canyons of the Navajo National Monument near Kayenta. The forms are somber and tragic under his hand (Fig. 3). Only across grand, unlovely Chaco does he let the vast, bright sky sweep wide, its cumulus taking shape in puffs of heat off the desert floor (Fig. 4). Here his instinct for space and breadth is surely right, because Chaco Canyon, now a desiccated furnace (Fig. 5), was of all Pueblo sites the most culturally imperial, fed by vast cornfields, heavily populated, and majestic in its architectural forms. What in religion and architecture may have filtered up to Chaco from the far-off Mexican south in its most northerly expansive Toltec-Chichimec days of the tenth through the twelfth centuries, and what might have been passed on therefrom even to the great Mesa Verde, are matters for discussion and dispute; but the communal grandeur which human aspiration once achieved there is perfectly clear in its ruins.

Current makes us feel a special kind of heroism in that collective effort (Fig. 6). He shows us the man-made walls rising totally free of the canyon's sides, almost rivalling them in height. He swings his camera up into obsessively clear focus on the outer wall of Pueblo Bonito and notes the pressures of life across the centuries there in the varieties of masonry, blocked doorways, and closed-up windows (Fig. 7). The walls, with their cores of mud and rubble and their exactly fitted surfaces of blocks and wafers of stone, turn away from the cliff, diminishing in width as they rise, and enclose a complex labyrinth of their own (Figs. 8, 9). Curiously enough, Current never helps us to apprehend the elaborate organization of rectangular rooms and circular kivas in the great buildings of the Chaco, though he does give us a rather unsatisfactory view of one of the so-called Great Kivas in Pueblo Bonito (Fig. 10). Nor does he show us the clear, overall shapes of those buildings: the gigantic *D* of Pueblo Bonito, the embracing wings of the Pueblo del Arroyo, or the generous sweep of the colonnaded courtyard in Chetro Ketl. In fact, his best focus is a truly obsessive one, perhaps like that of most of the people who built the pueblos: it is upon the individual structural unit, the single piece of stone (Fig. 11). There is a good deal of anthropological truth in this as well, since it emphasizes the generally democratic and egalitarian organization of the prehistoric no less than the modern pueblos. The masonry is neither of huge blocks dragged in by gangs of workmen like that of Egypt, nor of superbly finished monumental units cut by individual sculptors like that of Greece, but of brick-sized slabs and handfuls of small tabular stones, carried by cooperating groups of moderately skilled individual men and, probably, women. The surface mosaic so fashioned over a rubble core totally lacks the figural imagery of the Mayan technique, which it otherwise recalls. Nor are the units mass-produced, like the very similar *opus incertum* of Rome. Every inch of every wall is different, whether in the precise patterns of Pueblo Bonito or Casa Rinconada or the generally rougher fluidities of Chetro Ketl (Figs. 12, 13). There is, of course, a development across time as well, but the communal discipline involved always remains a very Indian one, creating a complex order infinitely particularized but deceptively offhand.

Still close up, Current shows us the other major elements of structure: the round beams of ponderosa pine, which made the multifloor levels possible, tied the walls together, and served as lintels for the doors (Figs. 14, 15, 16). These led *en suite* from room to room, forming a hive of rectangular volumes, some buried deep in the building, cut off from light. But they were balanced by rooftop terraces and complemented by ceremonial kivas. Those cylindrical chambers were dug into the ground or built up behind rectangular outer shells and packed around with the sanctifying earth. To see them properly in Current's photographs we must go with him to the pueblo at Aztec (Figs. 17, 18). That site was equidistant from Chaco Canyon and the Mesa Verde and was influenced by both. It has a Great Kiva in the courtyard, in a position recalling one at Chetro Ketl, but its masonry resembles that of the Mesa Verde, with chunkier blocks and fewer small tabular stones.

An almost delirious rhythm of rectangle and circle, of dwelling room and kiva, was characteristic of fully developed Great Pueblo architecture at the Mesa Verde no less than in Chaco Canyon. But, during the thirteenth century, their last of residence at that site, many of the inhabitants of the Mesa Verde abandoned their homes on the mesa tops (though not the fields of corn, beans, and squash upon them) and built their living units into the caverns and along the ledges of the canyon walls. Later pueblos, such as those at Puye, Tsankawi, and El Rito de los Frijoles on the Pajarito Plateau above the Rio Grande, made a common practice of occupying both the mesa tops and the caves along their sides at one and the same time. It is possible that an increased need for protection from scattered nomad marauders, or more likely from each other, may have played a part in the movement of the

Anasazi to the cliffs at Mesa Verde, but it may also have been intended to serve a ritual purpose during a time of cultural upheaval and increasing drought, and it clearly coincided with an enriched ceremonial development of the architecture as a whole. In fact, new ceremonial structures, like "Sun Temple" and others, were made to crown the ridges and the rocky edges of the mesas. A semi—Great Kiva, called "Fire Temple," was built in a cleft. Perhaps the larger cliff dwellings, too, had special sanctity. Kivas proliferated in them, and they were joined by high towers, some circular, others rectangular (Figs. 19, 20, 21, 22). Current is especially eloquent here. In his photographs, Cliff Palace is seen massing actively upward in solid masonry like an Italian medieval town, climbing the hill slope, riding the reefs of rock, culminating in towers. Yet everything has its own fixed sky in the canopy of living rock above. Toward it the towers lift, the kivas with their *sipapu* and fire altars plunge below, and the two complementary opposites of kiva and tower are often linked by passageways, as if they were exploring the environment between them, making multiple contact with the earth (Fig. 22).

The urban pattern as a whole is a dense and intense one. It is examined in Current's photographs of Spruce Tree House as well (Figs. 23–28). The kiva tops were roofed over, forming plazas, dance platforms. Through them the aggressive ladder poles lifted (Figs. 27, 28) ; up these, through the smoke, climbed the men, masked as gods, or messengers of the gods, or animals whose lives are linked to men. They must have danced upon the kivas as upon drums. The whole town would have throbbed as one body, the despair of homeless barbarians, where men knew how to make things work, the place of psychic power, here wholly tapping the powers of earth as well. The women, too, probably had some part in the kivas and a large part in many of the dances, as they do among the Pueblos today, but they would also have watched from the rooftops and from the doorways like eyes (Figs. 23, 24, 27, 28). Actors and spectators were tensely linked. In Current's rather theatrical photographs the towns remind us, as they can hardly help but do, of the vibrant stages for human action—the exactly scaled streets and room volumes—which Giotto painted or, in ruin, of Maso's blasted townscapes in a plague-struck world (Figs. 25, 26, 29). The plaster with which some of the walls are still covered adds to an illusion at once surrealist and Italianate (Fig. 24), but the incomparable fourth court in Spruce Tree House shows us the fundamental kiva-and-courtyard structure of an urbanism which was unique to the Southwest (Fig. 28).

How much the ancient inhabitants of the Mesa were self-consciously aware of their sites as dramatic and emotionally stimulating ones is a matter of question. Certainly modern Pueblo Indians see themselves as living in harmony with natural features of which they are acutely aware. But there seems to be more than harmony here: challenge and response, bravado even, or sublimated fear. Current's photographs seize upon that vivid relationship between men and places. Balcony House fills its cleft with man-made hollows, tautly contained against the void (Figs. 29, 30, 31). In the photographs of Square Tower House (Figs. 32, 33), all the energies seem to go into that proud vertical element rising, backed against the cliff. A pyramid of room volumes once rose with it, all lifting directly toward an upward-bursting inverted pyramid of rock, so dramatizing the natural shape and, fragile under the overhanging cornices, seeming to assert a human capacity to contribute to the world. Here the man-made is in part supported by nature and in part comments upon it. Pure towers were built wholly self-supporting on the Mesa tops and near water sources in areas, such as Hovenweep, which were derivative from the Mesa Verde. They appear much less like fortresses than symbols of dominion or instruments of prayer, and they seem to stand at the very edge of a kind of humanistic expressionism in architecture to which the Indian, with the almost immediate retraction of Pueblo culture, never afterward aspired.

Again, it is hard to know what caused scores of medium-sized groups of buildings and hundreds of tiny groups to spread out vertiginously among the shallow caverns and narrow ledges of Mesa Verde's canyon walls. Perhaps their inhabitants were simply placing themselves boldly but as a matter of course between their precious farming terraces above and on the talus slopes below (Figs. 34–37). Current's photographs ask those questions with some awe, and they show characteristic cases where dwellings cling to almost vertical walls, while kivas group densely upon whatever platform for building is offered elsewhere (Figs. 36, 37). The high-volumed natural arch of Figure 37 is comparatively rare among the more generally strung-out clefts in the Mesa Verde's horizontal strata, but it is the characteristic shape in the frozen sand, wind hollowed, of the canyons which comprise the Navajo National Monument (perhaps misleadingly named) in Arizona. Figure 38 shows the landscape with acute sensitivity, Figure 39 the steep semidome in which the pueblo now called Betatakin was built. Here, as part of the scooped-out conformation of the sandstone, the floor of the cleft slopes upward much more sharply than in any of the Mesa Verde's major sites (Figs. 40, 41, 42). It billows cloudlike up and over, and the buildings cling to it, as if riding it, borne upward by it. Their walls are footed only by shallow, pecked steps in the rock and by friction. They hunch themselves up the slope. The restriction of their platform may have had something to do with the fact that the single ceremonial room found at Betatakin which is clearly a kiva is a square one (Figs. 42, 43). There are a couple of rooms which may have had ceremonial functions, but there must have been other obvious kivas. Were they on the talus below, as sometimes at Mesa Verde, now perhaps covered by a rock fall, and were they round? Rectangular kivas had begun to appear in some of the Mesa Verde's smaller clefts. Elsewhere at Kayenta, as in Keet Seel, there were kivas both round and square, the latter sometimes called *kihus*. The Hopi, who are in every likelihood the descendants of the Anasazi of this region, use only rectangular kivas today.

The architecture of Betatakin seems generally later in date than that of the Mesa Verde, and it was rapidly constructed and soon abandoned, probably all in the late thirteenth century, while drought was beginning to empty the entire area. It is built of a much more casual masonry than was normal at the older sites (Fig. 44), with rudely shaped stones, large swatches of mud mortar, and ragged profiles. There is much less interplay between the natural and the man-made; the constructed forms simply occupy the natural shape, which becomes their single monumental insignia. They are small in relation to it. The contrast with the free-standing, monumental shapes of the apartment buildings in Chaco Canyon is total. Now the hollow of the natural arch can remind modern viewers of one of Buckminster Fuller's geodesic domes, an environmental envelope in which the protected living units can spread out quite loosely. Here, however, each natural vault is different, forming a unique and, one can hardly help but feel, valued shape for each pueblo. Inscription House, which is also in Navajo National Monument, wings out like a bird (Fig. 45). Keet Seel, not far from Betatakin, swims sleekly through the cliff, lifting a fat tail (Fig. 46). But its white ceiling, streaked by water scourings, swells out and down like a ballooning sail. Everything is subordinate to the rush and sweep of that canopy, swirling over the pueblo as its own low-hanging, stormy sky (Figs. 47, 48). Under it, the buildings are marvelously preserved from the weather and are strung out with an apparent dispersion of grouping and casualness of fabric (Fig. 49). Compared with Cliff Palace or Spruce Tree House, the group is almost suburbanized and so prefigures modern pueblo architecture which, in common with that of its continent as a whole, shows persistent suburban tendencies. At Keet Seel, one is reminded in every way of most contemporary pueblos, those along the Rio Grande as well as those of the Hopi. The usual elements are all there: a mixture of rubble or adobe masonry with jacal, wattle-and-daub work (Figs. 50, 51), unemphatic massing, irregular roof lines, abandoned rooms, and scattered poles pointing toward the sky (Fig. 52). Current's photograph here is correctly touching and rather sad.

I do not mean to suggest by this that modern pueblos have given up the essential core of their ceremonial life. It is their glory that they have manifestly not done so. But the intensity of their ritual is, on the whole, much less embodied in their architecture than heretofore; their buildings and villages have, in a physical sense, become culturally minimal, as if now intended to serve as hardly more than deceptively simple settings for their great dances—for, that is, their people's ritual behavior in the landscape. But they do indeed furnish such settings and are therefore still wholly alive.

We are brought back to a prehistoric intensity of architectural-natural feeling in Current's hallucinatory photographs of the Canyon de Chelly (Figs. 2, 53–65). That rose-red miracle of peace and silence is washed by a shallow, spreading stream deep down below the windy mesa height. It is now the heart of the Navajo Reservation. Sheep bells echo far off in it, and painted ponies run free over the bright sands and through the thin leaves' quiver. Here are some of the oldest ruins in the Anasazi area, but the major cliff dwellings are contemporary with those of Chaco Canyon and the Mesa Verde, and many of them were reoccupied by Hopi clans at a much later date. For the Navajo, too, the canyon became a refuge and a sacred place. It was planted with their beloved fruit trees, inherited from the Spanish through the Hopi, until the United States Army cut them all down.

So dreamlike is the site that we can hardly help but see the ruins in part out of their immediate cultural context, and Current indeed makes us perceive them as images of timeless experience. Foremost among them, the White House seems both to exploit the cliff (Fig. 55) and to be consumed by it as by the great white whale (Figs. 56, 57). A talus unit of rooms and round kivas rises toward it out of the delicate grove on the canyon floor, while the cliff grinds down upon it and out of the toothed shadow the white-stuccoed wall gleams. Tiny it is in relation to the whole canyon wall, quiet, engulfed, and far away. Yet, like a majority of the ruins in the Canyon de Chelly and its connected Canyon del Muerto, the White House is sited for a view straight down the stream. Current's photographs do not show those relationships, but the cliffs indeed deploy before most of the remains like classic forecourts of an unearthly red splendor, grander than Palladian (Figs. 58, 59). Arabian Petra is in some sense recalled, but here the blessing of the river glistens to cool and soften the scene. The effect is of country houses with fine plantations, exploiting the place, though there are few vast vaults to spread out within as at Kayenta. Only in Mummy Cave, not shown by Current, or in nearby Three-Turkey Canyon, does that feature reappear. Three-Turkey Ruin climbs at several levels within its ample hollow (Fig. 60). It has one rounded structure that recalls the towers of Hovenweep or the Mesa Verde (Fig. 61), but on the whole it is simply a gentle Hopi town. In Current's close-up it becomes a model: scaleless, breathless, lonely.

Not far from the entrance to Canyon del Muerto the cliff is undercut to provide a protected space for building under its inclined plane. There Antelope House stands largely free of the rock, rising to a three-storied tower that can, in part, recall those of the Mesa Verde or even Chaco Canyon's high free-standing walls (Figs. 62, 63). But here the cliff engulfs it, and Current presents it to us in that way as a ruin eaten up by time, lost in nature's vastness. The photographs are darkened, melancholy, but not unbearably or meaninglessly so. They are historically apt enough, indicating human loss and change. Current shows us Navajo animal paintings rising above the trees on the canyon wall nearby (Fig. 64), because here, as throughout so much of their former area, the pueblos were eventually abandoned, and the Anasazi, leaving their petroglyphs of men and animals—of horned beings, humpbacked flute players, sky altars, turtles, and sacred snakes—gave way before, though they were never wholly unreverenced by, Navajo horsemen (Fig. 65) sweeping the land.

Fig. 1. Chaco Canyon, New Mexico. Pueblo Bonito. Detail

Current's sharp focus emphasizes each wafer of stone and picks out at least three different periods of construction. Two fundamental approaches toward building a door are shown: functional above (wider for the upper body and its burdens), structural below (narrower at the top to reduce the span).

Fig. 2. Canyon de Chelly, Arizona. General View

Current makes the sandstone walls near Spider Rock look like the gnarled roots of the earth. His dark printing in black and white stresses the canyon's awesome sculptural presence rather than the warm red-pink glow which actually softens its effect.

Fig. 3. Kayenta, Arizona. Navajo National Monument. General View of Canyon from Above

Current makes the most of the deceptive scale of this canyon system, which shelters a number of major ruins. It is a long way down from the wind-shaped, enormously proportioned sandstone bosses of the cliffs to the trees in the depths.

Fig. 4. Chaco Canyon. General View

Current gets some sense of the amplitude of a site which has so far proved hard to photograph properly. Many great community houses lie under the cliffs, while the always-widening cut of the arroyo can just be made out in the middle distance. The tragedy of desiccation is obvious. Pines once grew here.

Fig. 5. Chaco Canyon. Detail of Canyon Wall

Exfoliation has strewn blocks and slabs across the talus as if they
had been scattered by giants. One is somewhat reminded of the
rock formations which crown the passes into the Argolid. Chaco
has its own Cyclopean scale.

Fig. 6. Chaco Canyon. Pueblo Bonito. Five-Storied Wall and Cliff from the South

This noble photograph makes the wall rear up to challenge the looming natural forms. Different masonry types are apparent, as is the use of wooden beams for rafters and lintels. The wall thins as it rises.

Fig. 7. Pueblo Bonito. Five-Storied Wall. Exterior Face

The focus of this view of the wall from the outside picks up the faces of the larger stones and seems to make them swim like a many-tiered school of fish through an ocean of tabular wafers. It also dramatizes the use of extended lintels to provide tensile strength and to tie two openings together. Similar details were developed for brick and concrete by LeCorbusier in the nineteen fifties.

Fig. 8. Pueblo Bonito. East Wall and Cliff

This photograph rivals Figure 6 in grandeur and makes the hollows
of the structure and the protective embrace of the exterior wall even
more evident. Some of the blocks from the section of cliff which
collapsed onto Pueblo Bonito in the early twentieth century are
just visible in the rear. Current picks up a rhythmic relationship
between the profiles of the cliff and that of the ruined walls.

Fig. 9. Pueblo Bonito. Southeast Corner

Here again Current makes us perceive the heroic quality of the building and the magnitude of the communal task, which is reflected in the endless shoals of small masonry units. These are laid up dry, fitted perfectly together over an inner core of rubble and mud. One of the corner doorways, constructed on a kind of squinchlike diagonal, is shown at the left.

Fig. 10. Pueblo Bonito. Great Kiva

Current's photograph gives some idea of the size of this Great Kiva but little of its location. It is set about at the focal point of the whole complex, between the two major courtyards and close to the southern wall. Foot drums (?), benches, and storage niches can be seen.

Fig. 11. Chaco Canyon. Wall Mosaics

The type above is common in the Pueblo Bonito, that below in the so-called Casa Rinconada. The latter is a Great Kiva set by itself in a topographically central location directly across the canyon from Pueblo Bonito.

Fig. 12. Chaco Canyon. Chetro Ketl. Long Wall. Detail

The greater number of flat tabular stones and the generally long
and rather irregular larger blocks give a looser and more fluid look
to the masonry of this ruin. Windows, beams, and an unusually
articulated floor-level detail are also shown.

Fig. 13. Chetro Ketl. Long Wall

Here the windows and string-course shown in Figure 12 unite to give the effect of a designed façade, with a rather regular rhythm of openings and a kind of median cornice line. Can influence from Toltec Mexico, apparent elsewhere in Chetro Ketl, be surmised here as well?

Fig. 14. Pueblo Bonito. Wall and Beam-ends

Current dramatizes the intense contrasts of shape and texture where
the cylindrical beams of ponderosa pine are at once supported and
engulfed by an ocean of tabular stones. These are found and broken
off as necessary but not cut.

Fig. 15. Pueblo Bonito. Interior Doorway

The scale of a room: a doorway just big enough to bend easily through, a ceiling just high enough to allow a man to stand upright and touch the thin sticks which span as a ceiling between the beams and upon which the packed mud of the upper floor is placed.

Fig. 16. Pueblo Bonito. Rooms *en Suite*

As at Versailles, the living apartments are served not by corridors but by communicating doorways. Communal living provided for little privacy in either case, and the spatial vistas created are impressive. There is always the presentiment of an imminent appearance.

Fig. 17. Aztec National Monument, New Mexico. Kivas in Main Block

These sacred chambers were built up and then packed around with earth, unlike the Great Kiva in the courtyard at Aztec, the upper part of which was permitted to project above ground.

Fig. 18. Aztec. Kivas. Detail

Like Aztec itself, the masonry here is midway between that of Chaco Canyon and Mesa Verde. Some of Chaco's small tabular stones are present but the more uniform larger blocks of Mesa Verde clearly dominate. The photograph engulfs us in the building, largely because Current here uses the device of joining two square prints to achieve a more complete and realistic sense of space as the human eye actually perceives it.

Fig. 19. Mesa Verde, Colorado. Cliff Palace. General View Looking South

There has been some reconstruction and stabilization since the ruins were
discovered in the nineteenth century. This is an expressive photograph of the
largest of the cliff dwellings at Mesa Verde. The giant presence of the cliff is
made to set off the crystalline geometry of the man-made forms. It is another
of Current's heroic views.

Fig. 20. Cliff Palace. View Looking North

Here the pressure of the cliff is felt, as well as the depth of its cleft.
Kivas are built up forward, living rooms behind, storage deepest in.

Fig. 21. Cliff Palace. Kivas and Cylindrical Tower

The kivas were of course originally roofed over, with an entrance smoke hole in the ceiling. Their association with towers is a fairly late development at Mesa Verde, and some isolated kiva-tower units, like special temples, were built on the mesa tops above the cliff dwellings.

Fig. 22. Cliff Palace. Kivas and Rectangular Towers

Some of the original white plaster still adheres to the tower, and
some painting can be seen on its interior walls. Here Mesa Verde's
great rhythm of rectangles and circles shows more clearly than in
any of Current's other photographs.

Fig. 23. Spruce Tree House. General View of First and Second Courts

This ruin is the second largest of those so far excavated at Mesa Verde. The cliff entirely dominates in this view, with the stuccoed wall fragile beneath it.

Fig. 24. Spruce Tree House. First Court. Plastered Wall

Current's lighting is dramatic here as he contrasts the light-colored
plaster, beautifully crackled, with the black apertures in the wall
face. The larger are doors; the smaller, windows.

Fig. 25. Spruce Tree House. Third Court. Rooms and Kivas

Here the volumes of space are read as in a stage set: the hollow cylinder of the kiva, the two-storied near-cubes of dwelling rooms, the keyhole doorway. The close relationship of these environmental elements to human size recalls the volumes of space created as a setting for human action in fourteenth-century Italian paintings.

Fig. 26. Spruce Tree House. Third Court. Keyhole Doorways and Balcony

Current again dramatizes the contrasts of value in an eminently
pictorial way and especially recalls the planes of ruined wall which
define the space in a number of late-medieval frescoes.

Fig. 27. Spruce Tree House. Kiva Detail and Fifth Court Detail

The two worlds of life in the pueblo are shown here: the lower world of the kiva with its hearth, draft screen, and air vent (called a spirit hole by the Indians themselves), and the upper world of emergence through the smoke into the beautifully paved urban plaza which is formed by the kiva's roof. The small hole in the floor, which was called the *sipapu*, a means of spiritual connection with an even lower world, was normally on a line with the hearth and is not shown in this photograph.

Fig. 28. Spruce Tree House. Fourth Court. Kiva Ladder; Doors, Windows, Stone Lintels, and Wooden Balcony Beams

Up these ladders climbed the masked dancers, watched by the townspeople in the doorways and on the balconies. The high ladder poles dramatized that intensely urban relationship. It is as if the gods burst upward out of the earth in the center of the Campidoglio.

Fig. 29. Mesa Verde. Balcony House

This moderate-sized ruin had a high wall to protect its inhabitants from the precipitous drop before it. Here the natural rock, the rough boulders, and the bricklike stones show a progression from natural to man shaped which is a little like that to be seen in the western bastion of the Athenian Acropolis.

Fig. 30. Balcony House. Retaining Wall and Kivas

The walls in Mesa Verde are much thinner than those in Chaco Canyon. The individual blocks are generally two-hand sized ("loaf shaped," one observer expressively called them), and they are bonded with generous amounts of mud mortar.

Fig. 31. Balcony House. Detail

Current makes this wall look like a mask. It is clearly a modern dramatization, but one should be wary of supposing that the Indians never intended such effects or imbodiments.

Fig. 32. Mesa Verde. Square Tower House. Detail

This photograph reads like a blow-up of Figure 33, which follows. Current delights in such changes of scale. Here he shows us how the great house rose in steps from the kivas to the tower, which sets its feet on the gigantic boulder in the center.

Fig. 33. Square Tower House. General View

A haunting photograph, where Current helps us to perceive the
pueblo climbing up the fault in the cliff, which then billows out
above it to the mesa top.

Fig. 34. Mesa Verde. Long House. Detail

These kivas are circular, but one can see why some of the smaller
settlements in Mesa Verde began to employ rectangular types.
The footing was sometimes very restricted indeed.

Fig. 35. Long House. General View

In this view Current shows us more of the whole structure of the canyon in Mesa Verde, from the wooded talus slope up the streaked cliff face to the mesa top.

Fig. 36. Mesa Verde. Mummy House

Current shows a real respect for the tenacity of the builders of some
of the smaller cliff dwellings. He extracts from the view some sense
of participation in a rite, wherein humanity entrusts itself wholly
to the terror and majesty of the earth.

Fig. 37. Mesa Verde. Mug House

A compact group of kivas with rectangular and cylindrical towers,
all set within a low vault above which a monumental arch swings.
Some tiny units explore the crevice.

Fig. 38. Kayenta. Navajo National Monument. Canyon Wall opposite Betatakin

Current derives a silvery texture from foliage, tree trunks, and sandstone alike. The photograph gives a fine sense of what it feels like
to inhabit a cliff dwelling which looks out to the opposite face of a
canyon. The whole environment becomes one building at a scale
which the nineteenth century would surely have described as sub-
lime.

Fig. 39. Navajo National Monument. Betatakin from across the Canyon

Here the tremendous scale of the earth which Current suggested in
Figure 3 is emphasized by the introduction into it of its tiny human
component: the cliff dwelling lost within the most architectural of natural arches, rising as between great watchtowers or bastions to the
sloping roof of the mesa top. It is all one monumental shape. Current
uses it grandly to introduce one of his most moving architectural se-
quences, an exploration of the relationship between nature and mankind
at Betatakin.

Fig. 40. Betatakin. General View

This view, as Current develops it, becomes an expression of the precarious setting that nature offers for human life. The cliff is alive and enormous in its sweeping shapes, which toss like the great bulls at Lascaux. The man-made cubes are tight and pinched beneath them. There is indeed quite the same feeling that the running animals of paleolithic cave paintings inspire: of primitive men not counting themselves as much in comparison with the unwearying energy which the earth and its immortal nations of animals embodied.

Fig. 41. Betatakin. Principal Group

Here, in contrast to Figure 40, emphasis is on the proud massing of
the human settlement. Its walls lift boldly in rising tiers ; the beams
make a brave show as they project into the void.

Fig. 42. Betatakin. Walls and Slope

The walls mount the cliff like mountain climbers; holes are pecked out for their footings. The masonry resembles that of Mesa Verde but is somewhat rougher, with more irregular blocks and rubble infill.

Fig. 43. Betatakin. Rooms and Courtyard. Masonry and Jacal

A roof opening in what may have been a rectangular sacred chamber; separated by a courtyard from a building of which the non-bearing wall is jacal (wattle-and-daub) construction, with a beautiful cedar beam still supported by the masonry walls which frame it.

Fig. 44. Betatakin. Wall Construction

These views of the upper, smaller house group in Betatakin clearly show the elongated, sometimes irregularly shaped blocks and the thick layers of mortar in which broken stones are embedded.

Fig. 45. Navajo National Monument. Inscription House

This fairly large ruin is located some miles west of Betatakin and is housed within one of the most spectacular of the natural cliff shapes, one which swings out and upward like a vast sounding board or, as Current shows us here, like a hollow in one of Henry Moore's earth-mother figures.

Fig. 46. Navajo National Monument. Keet Seel. From the Canyon Floor

Here the whole shape seems to swim through the cliff, which again, as at Betatakin, swings forward from its concave center to enormous bastions on both sides. The water streaking which is noticeable in all the caves of this area is especially dramatic here, and Current makes the most of it. He also shows us the canyon floor, so making us sense what it must have been like for the Anasazi to approach such a monumental shape as a home.

Fig. 47. Keet Seel. General View

Current's technique of putting two frames side by side in order to approximate the actual wide arc of human vision normally produces less distortion than a single wide-angle view. Here it is essential in order to capture the full billow of the cliff which is Keet Seel's glory.

Fig. 48. Keet Seel. Retaining Wall and Cavern Roof, Looking West

The cliff ceiling is much lower than at Betatakin. It swoops down over the pueblo and gives it almost total protection from the weather.

Fig. 49. Keet Seel. View Eastward

The grouping is looser than at Betatakin and much more spread out than was common in Mesa Verde. The resemblance to a modern Hopi town is very obvious. Note should be taken of the fact that the tower-building instinct, so strong at Mesa Verde, seems to have passed by. The town is humble.

Fig. 50. Keet Seel. Masonry

The stones are smaller and rougher than those at Betatakin, and the rubble mortar is larger in area. Contrast should be made with the fine tabular masonry of Chaco and the substantial blocks of Mesa Verde. Whether the change should be read as the deterioration of a technique or the development of another may be open to question. Keet Seel stands in relation to the earlier sites much as Roman rubble-concrete construction does to Greek finely cut masonry.

Fig. 51. Keet Seel. Jacal

Jacal is a technique older than Egypt, and some of Egypt's major architectural forms in stone grew out of it. Among the Anasazi it also reflected old traditions but produced no symbolic holdovers in Pueblo masonry construction. At the same time, as for example in Egypt to the present day, it continued to be used for minor structures.

Fig. 52. Keet Seel. Detail of Eastern Section

The importance of wood in the general architectural environment of contemporary pueblos is well suggested here. The ladders have now generally been abandoned, except for kivas, but the projecting beams and especially the extensive corrals, often built of vertical poles, still abound. Their skeletal shapes expressively complement the masonry or adobe blocks of the houses. The wind sweeps upward through a cliff face like sky.

Fig. 53. Canyon de Chelly. Rio de Chelly and Canyon Wall

In one of his most sensitive photographs Current captures something of the sweetness of the canyon with its gentle contrasts of
light, shade, and texture. The river washes in wide shallows through
most of the canyon and, under normal conditions, disappears into
the sands before reaching its mouth.

Fig. 54. Canyon de Chelly. Sun on the River

Current must have been visiting the White House, shown in the following photographs. This section of river is near it and can run with considerable force, changing its channel and sometimes peeling away the low banks that can be seen in the distance. A Navajo farm lies beyond the trees.

Fig. 55. Canyon de Chelly. The White House in the Canyon Wall

Current again dramatizes the contrast in scale between natural forms and human building. He uses the streaking of the rose-red cliff to suggest cosmic forces beating down on the pueblo. He suggests the lovely grove which stands below the cleft, but the general effect is of a gigantic Navajo blanket.

Fig. 56. White House with Lower Structure

The dwelling units and kivas on the canyon floor were once connected with the group in the cleft. The white wall is stucco. Current
here makes the cliff look like a sperm whale, with its flat lower jaw
and enormous head. Certainly he dramatizes the swallowing of the
pueblo by it. A number of Anasazi petroglyphs can be seen.

Fig. 57. White House. Detail

Again, a study in pressure and transcendence. Current causes the
structures to flaunt the cliff like a great pediment.

Fig. 58. Canyon del Muerto. Ruin No. 10 (Mindeleff)

The Canyon del Muerto forks off toward the east from the Canyon de Chelly. It was named for one of its clefts in which a number of Navajo were massacred by the Spanish. It, too, contains many ruins set at all heights in the canyon walls.

Fig. 59. Canyon de Chelly. Ruin No. 16 (Mindeleff)

One of the smaller ruins. Current makes the rock run and rear like surf.

Fig. 60. Three-Turkey Canyon. Three-Turkey Ruin from the Opposite
Rim of the Canyon

This canyon can be reached by a rough road along the mesa top
from the rim of the Canyon de Chelly. Its sandstone formations
tend to be somewhat more broken up than the great sweeps of
cliff in the other canyons. In this photograph it looks like wood
carving.

Fig. 61. Three-Turkey Ruin

Current again zooms us in close. The association of cubes with curved walls and the placement of the voids and the roof terraces recall early twentieth-century studies of villas by LeCorbusier. That most influential of modern architects, who so lovingly studied the traditional architecture of the Mediterranean basin, would undoubtedly have admired Anasazi architecture equally well if he had ever had the chance to know it.

Fig. 62. Canyon del Muerto. Antelope House

This ruin stands on the canyon floor under a slanted cliff, again looking like a sky. The two larger petroglyphs in this view are probably juxtaposing two of the commonest animals of the Southwest, a rabbit and a lizard (very manlike except for the tail). The drawing is lively, even witty. Human hands, often found in the paleolithic caves of Europe, can be seen engraved on the wall at the lower left.

Fig. 63. Antelope House from Below

Another generous sweep of cliff at celestial scale. More petroglyphs can be seen.

Fig. 64. Canyon del Muerto. Navajo Paintings near Antelope House

The Hopi reoccupied some of the ruins in these canyons long after
their Anasazi ancestors had left them. The last of the Hopi were
evicted by the Navajo, to whom the canyon also became a loved
and holy sanctuary. Their paintings were surely influenced by the
old Anasazi petroglyphs but lack their curious, lively wit. The
photograph here is Current's most Japanese.

Fig. 65. Canyon de Chelly. Navajo Petroglyphs

These figures stand at a key point in the canyon where it is at its widest and makes a great bend. They seem to celebrate that moment of release with their headlong movement, but they also symbolize the end of a long era, that of the Anasazi before the horse came to the Southwest and changed its patterns of power. One is reminded of nineteenth-century Bushman rock paintings in South Africa, where mounted white hunters are all too easily slaughtering the eland, once a god.

657965

657965